CURB

CURB

DIVYA VICTOR

Nightboat Books
New York

ISBN: 978-1-64362-070-1

Cover design by Karin Aue
Text design and typesetting by HR Hegnauer
Text set in Avenir and Sabon

Cataloging-in-publication data is available from the Library of Congress

Nightboat Books
New York
www.nightboat.org

CONTENTS

This book was made to witness the following irreducible facts: these men once lived; they loved; they were loved; the United States of America is responsible for the force of feeling and action that ended their lives.

May their names never be forgotten.

BALBIR SINGH SODHI   MESA, ARIZONA

NAVROZE MODY   JERSEY CITY, NEW JERSEY

SRINIVAS KUCHIBHOTLA   OLATHE, KANSAS

SUNANDO SEN   QUEENS, NEW YORK

.

_____ , since you asked:

yes; I am
afraid all
the time; all
the places are all
the same to me; all
of us are the same to all
of them; this is all
that matters; all
of us don't matter at all.

           — My mother, as we pull my child
in a Radio Flyer wagon painted Cinnabar or
Hemoglobin. We are dragging all that blood around
in the afternoon with the fear
set soft in limbs roving the sidewalks
o'er the land of the free & the home of the brave.

SETTLEMENT

Settlers, over the land, over the sea
over the tile, over the stone floors
settlers over the furs, over the pinewood planks
of the house settled, the houses settled into the ground
the houses so buried; settling
pulling life like splinters
from the toboggans & caravans pulling cargo
settled out of suitcases, settled down
we settled in & so settled we
into our ways & with those ways did we settle
for this emptying of history
for this sternum rent in two
for this conscience as quiet
as the snap of a wishbone
sucked white.

HEDGES

Through the skin, the world & the body touch, defining their common border (edge). Contingency means mutual touching (common tangency).

—Michel Serres, *The Five Senses*

first there was a sea

& then there was a knot of hair

first there was a line

& then there was a story

how do the dead wait
in this tunnel
this tomb of book & breast
patient

1.

at the consulate, the line
for birth certificates is the line
for death certificates

        was the child born beyond a boundary?
        was the boundary wrought in gunmetal & grain?

when they pull her out
the trundle of my pelvis
rattles   (but doesn't give way)
in the prattle of the operating theatre
she arrives like a slap
backwards, fleeing the face, the palm indigo
smarting from flight. Our shared border is a fist
unfurling; a red flag
        her, a thing pink
        found in the maraud
taken as a peel is, further & further from the fruit
until plum descends to plumb,
until a sound, long & lean, turns into a kind of skin
        her, a thing inked
        fleeced by charter

        were the parents held by the law?
        FS-240
        did they love in the same language?
        DS-1350

they first lift
serosa from serosa
arouse all the roses, prick each thorn
hum *sub rosa*
a song known to someone born
before you

aari   *ro*   *ari*   *raro*
             aari   *ro*   *ari*   *raro*
aararo *ari*   *ra ro*

2.

to pleach a tree, we take the dead
stem & braid it to a living branch
until a hedge thickens
until the braids come undone & the schoolyard
dusts black hair red
until, at the hospital ward, my cries command
the clouds to the window

                cumulus   alluvial   lunatic

each breath quests a gust, counts to five
makes a list of the names for god
twin simoons strand us both at the tear
where earth parts from earth

ज़मीन, our zikr; کڈ, our partition
awaking to daylight assembly
from one, many
ex ovum pluribus
us   *us*
strung on suture
a flag drying   saffron &   egg white &   succulent
on a clothes line

aloe, an organ; saffron, an ovary

patient's water intact, 48 hours later
they sweep the membrane of the water sac
they bring the sky broom
to enter my stoop
they bring the blocks of ice

                                        yes, I feel that
place them against my chest
                                        yes, I feel that

            she's ready

            unfold the shroud
            stanch the incision
            & sign here

                                aari   *ro*   *ari*   *raro*
                    aari   *ro*   *ari*   *raro*
aararo *ari*   *ra ro*

11

3.

until I was eleven, I slept
inside my mother's passport

in that photograph, I wear the face
which drank the wet moons, horns & all. I have the eyes
of a deer crossing the pacific
two stitches on a single stave.
stitch   stitch
                  this will form a good scar
                  this will be a ring of, ring of roses
                  a pocket full of passport poses

do you have proof of identity?
                  she is her mother's child as I am
                  my mother's child & as she is her mother's
                                          aari   ro   ari
                              raro
aari   ro   ari   raro
                              aararo ari   ra ro
                              aari   ro   ari   raro
                                                  aari   ro   ari
          raro   aararo
          ari   ra ro

hang the towels, beat the rugs, skim the whey
swaddle the archipelagos
we are coming home with the bundled papers
we have fledged ourselves
over this line
paper cranes that we are, in this bleach sky

this is the plot:
as in, we now have a story
as in, I pricked it red
where you & I meet
on a grid of wet
as in, I have made a notarized copy
of all our feathers

PLOTS

A philosophy of the street in which nothing happens, outwardly.
—Bhanu Kapil, *Ban en Banlieue*

STOOP (DAMP)

We stand facing the children. The children stand facing away from each other. We are facing each other, taking turns to coo at each other about our children. So adorable, we are saying, & we turn away, & we face the children. On our stoops, we face away & towards the children. From the stoop, some grass is greener. From the stoop, she is saying something & she is looking at my daughter: look at those eyelashes, & look at that tan, & look at all that language that she will have. So adorable. The words roll down the verge & into the curb. The curb is still dark with the night rain. The neighbor facing our lawn walks over the verge with her Labrador. She is facing us & she is waving. Look at that coat, look at that happy wagging tail. So adorable, we are saying. We look up at the sky. We face down & to each end of the street. What a great day for a walk, we are saying. We turn away & we face the children.

STOOP (DRY)

from here & to the left,
for the doctor's house

> 12 minutes by foot with a backpack
> & then back to check the mailbox

from here & to the right,
for the music teacher's house

> 3 minutes by foot with a lunch box
> & then back to send the telegram

from here & to the north,
for the store which sells
two patties with ketchup

> 10 minutes on banana bike with
> empty clothbag & then back to buy
> more stamps

from here & to the south,
for the church with the small stone mary

> 8 minutes on moped with wine-
> offering on lap & then back to lick
> the envelopes

from here & to her feet,
for a dress damp with running

> so no time, so no luggage

from here & to the sky,
for a banyan older than this story

> so no time, so no luggage

for when they veer, the fathers
from here to there
far for a pittance
we veered with them
far for a memory of a him
at home with letters

LAWN (TEMPERATE)

The block party has two types of sausages. She meets two Bills, two Susans, two Phils, two Marys. These sausages look so good, she is saying, but she hasn't tasted them. Bill, Susan, Phil, Mary have grandchildren named Bill, Susan, Phil, & Mary. They face her, head cocked. Olivia? Vivian? Vivia? Diva? Tibia? "It's Teeveeya," one offers. "This. That," she tries. She gestures towards the sausages. So good, she is saying. Her name is small talk here. It is inclement weather, a store going out of business, an ongoing sale at the end of a season. It is one time something happened & boy was it something. She slips into the Midwestern apology, beer in hand: "There you go! You almost got it." She is laughing the same laugh that she has heard her father laugh at so many all white office parties, cheering their attempts, playing surrogate to their embarrassment, comforting them into peace in their mouths, where no tongue ever pressed against the teeth to create the sound of the soft D, the D of The, the D of Thee, the D of Then, the D of Therein, Therefore, & These, where no eyes have gaped as teeth moved & tongue lolled to find horizon, where no eyes have looked for ships seeking safe harbor in a perfect rounded sound, where no dock ever bobbed against that sweet thud of a velvet wavelet D, where no lip has ever parted to change the course for someone like me. So good, she is saying.

LAWN (ARID)

lawn of dust

you wash the keds on the yard stone
so our names are cleansed of spit

lawn of crow gather
& cow pause

you pick up the rolled newspaper
so our names arrive with the dawn

lawn of barefoot hopscotch

you touch the stick to the ground
so our names grow in the furrows

lawn of snail trail silver

you pin the dragonfly wings on the
barbs so our names are knotted with wire

lawn of weed & bramble

you toss the tennikoit across the street
so our names reach over their ears

lawn of badminton at midday

you dry the feathers on the clothesline
so our names take flight

lawn of milk

you walk with an empty pail to the gate
so our names are quenched

lawn of alert marigolds

you burn the camphor on the stoop
so our names are spelled in flames

lawn of red dirt at dusk

you sprinkle sugar on buttered bread
so our names are buried with yours

BEDS (CLAY)

We are on our knees. We are saying that the tulips have had it hard this week. We are saying something about the brightness & the dryness & we are saying we hope it will change. I press a finger into the loam, flick the dust on my jeans. We are listening to the snip of shears. I pick up a smooth, small disc of pink Sioux quartz, hold it like an avian heart in the palm. A disc slipped & beating from a time when all of North America was under sea. My finger walks the buttery vein that parses the stone in two & then in four. Its edges are under siege; its end at the foot of suburban perennials. Do you have stones, someone is asking me. Where you are from, do you have stones, like these? We have purple sunbirds, I am saying, & their hearts have four rooms, one for every answer to questions like these.

BEDS (RED LOAM)

for my father

in it we clip *it* comics

> Appa, our sheets are sails
> when those people came
> they trapped the wind that leaves your
> body behind

so we find a piece of *it* land

in it we clip *it* the postage stamps

> Papa, our letters are shirts
> when those people came
> they stripped the night that leaves your
> body behind

so we loosen the *it* soil

in it we clip *it* the obituaries

> Bapa, our names are masks
> when those people came
> they carve out the eyes that leave your
> body behind

so we dig the *it* damp

in it we clip *it* the headlines

> Naana, our rice is sand
> when those people came
> they filled the bowls that leave your
> body behind

so we peel back the *it* sod
in it we clip *it* the coupons

>Baba, our blood is water
>when those people came
>they drained the well that leaves your
>body behind

so we fill it with *it* sky
in it we clip *it* the tongue

>Abbaa, our cries are coups
>when those people come
>they will steal the sons who leave your
>body behind

Le moutonnement des haies/ C'est en moi que je l'ai.

The frothing of the hedges / I keep deep inside me.

Jean Wahl

NO ENGLISH.
INDIAN.
WALKING.

BLOOD / SOIL

Residential Neighborhood
Madison, Alabama

I slouch to the writing sideways
crab limbs cling to the torso in tumult
where my elbows bowl in, my knees keel
to my feet scraping off the carpet, frothing a writing body to the desk.
My reluctance is quicksand; this lyric lead. I can't know how
each fist knots, each knuckle locks

> his legs refuse gravity, legs coil on pavement
> his torso goes limp, keens quiet
> away from the dash-cam

> his head— its dread stillness

I said મેં કહ્યું   "No English. Indian. Walking"
I said મેં કહ્યું   "My handkerchief fell.
       I was brought down on the grass"

The Law says:
"To every action
there is always
an opposite & equal reaction"

therefore a handkerchief falls, therefore the shoulder blades blench
therefore they offer
his body to the sky, therefore heave it
weightless, therefore wrap it to the frame
because *he* is no matter; *he* is flinch, thin as linen, light *en plein air*
there is more
of him, more
where a skull folds
more where chest plows over, more where one body pushes
into another, pushes a therefore into asphalt
ploughs the life of blood & soil

therefore they hold it
here— \ a land dry as swatches of bone
here— \ drowned sound of flesh on the ground   hold it
here— \ land of more
                              >>HEY BUDDY

                              >>WHERE DO YOU LIVE?

                              >>WHERE YOU GOING?
a yard is a measure, a curb its end
this \ *is* how a landscape renders a portrait
as long & as wide as hemmed in history of linen
— was it white?
like the ones my father threw in the wash, soggy
from a day at the plant— or checkered? >>HEY BUDDY
like the cotton ones he picked for Sunday Mass—
or embroidered?

like the one in custody   >>HEY BUDDY
at the museum— a silk square with Krishna flanked
by gopis holding lilies blood-tipped
bone-white & buttered, its edges worn
from worry or waiting
or was it a measure of cotton slung around necks by Thugs—
to make a noose from a slung loop of a *rumāl*— a coin anointed
for Kali lashed
to one end & a life dwindling
at the other; to wrangle
a traveler
then strangle that stranger?

>>YOU WANNA STAND UP? *NO?*

>>YOU OK?

>>CAN YOU STAND UP?

>>YOU UNDERSTAND ENGLISH?

>>*NO?*

The Law says: "The mutual actions
of two bodies upon each other
are always equal,
& directed to contrary parts"
but his body was one of two
that couldn't speak of its place
therefore they swept leg under leg,
therefore made him look close at the land,
made him taste the verge between walk & veer

The Law says: "If you press a stone
with your finger, the finger
is also pressed
by the stone"
therefore, with these fingers, I will knot
a garland of buds plucked from the camphorweed
flailing on the curb where, cuffed
by the soft folds of his neck, his spine
snapped & swelled
& therefore we will wear its scratchy rope
for another century of stony sleep
until our sunder feels more like survival.

In February 2015, Sureshbhai Patel, 57, was visiting his son's family in Alabama, after recently becoming a grandfather. He was there to help care for his son's baby, who was born sooner than the family had anticipated. When he was taking a morning walk on his block, a neighbor had called the police, citing a "skinny black guy" prowling around the neighborhood. A cop car tracked him down, mere yards from his son's home. He was assaulted & thrown to the ground by Madison Police Officer Eric Parker. The assault left Patel paralyzed. The lawsuit against Parker alleged a number of claims: false arrest, improper search & seizure, use of excessive force. A year later, Parker was acquitted of civil rights charges & was reinstated into the Madison Police Force.

PETITIONS (FOR AN ALIEN RELATIVE)

Please do not include graphic photos of childbirth or intimate relations as evidence of a relationship or marriage.

—Special Instructions, Form I-130
(Petition for an Alien Relative),
  United States Citizenship and Immigration Services (USCIS)

FIRST PETITION

it is a Thursday
& no one out on this long street
looks like your mother
so you go home
wrap yourself in Form I-130
knit a nest with a ballpoint pen
limn your ken inside a placeholder
smooth your limbs into a square
to beg for a place for your first space
her
write a name into the petition, in thin
improbable syllables
       — no one calls her by this name, in the elsewhere
because they know her fish-market haggle:
purse tucked at the waist, sari pleats pulsing like flushed gills
       — no one, except the men
who will ask her *ma'am can you name two national holidays?*
& *ma'am, who lived in America before the Europeans arrived?*
so you plan it out, letter by letter in letters,
your mouth cupped to her cataracts
ma, just listen & answer the men who ask
how she came to know you, if she intends to remain here,
& *sir, for how long have you known*
that *ma* was a bowl made for two, brimming
beyond any border, red
as the arrival of her face seven years later,

a paper apparition drawn closer & closer to you by a queue
unknotting at a frayed horizon
in an airport
when
it is a Thursday
& suddenly she walks
through the passport photograph
you once stapled at the edge of a petition
to anchor her womb
to your migrating heart

SECOND PETITION

A.

Use this form if you are a citizen or lawful permanent resident (LPR) of the United States who needs to establish your relationship to an eligible relative who wishes to immigrate to the United States.

Write here, if you know this place as home, about a beloved whose skin you cannot live without; whose fingers know why the jasmine bushes will not flourish in your backyard in El Sobrante, why your batter sours too late, why no amount of sugar will make your tea sweet, why your front yard is scattered with pinions, why all mail arrives like a bird strike to the fuselage (the dotterels dawdling & then shredding the turbines); whose letters you fold & unfold until the creases give way & you put the pieces back together on the dining table— to make a map for a country made of vein & sinew with hands pulled clean of wedding bands & raw rice, a map for a country of two.

B.

If you need extra space to complete any section of this petition,
use the space provided in Part 9

Explain here, again, why they wish to leave behind the stone
well where they first kissed you; where the large terrapin laps the
shadow & circles around the mossy rock overhanging the clutch
of her eggs to circumnavigate a history of water trapped in land;
where ankles graze against cotton skirts stamped again, & again,
& again, with laughing doves carved into wooden blocks; where
an open suitcase is an undug grave; where a field of sugarcane is
a bruise spreading purple through land owned by the IMF, a land
free of flags, yet flagging, flagging, flagging.

THIRD PETITION

I am filing this petition for my (Select only one box):
- ☐ *Spouse*
- ☐ *Parent*
- ☐ *Brother/Sister*
- ☐ *Child*
- ☐ I am filing this petition during the third shift at the Mobil, I am filing a petition for her eyes & her tendency to leave jars open *That will be $4.50 Have a good one.* I am filing a petition for her eyes & her tendency to leave jars open & the way a nape turning away from me *That will be $17.80. Have a good one.* I am filing a petition for her eyes & her tendency to leave jars open & the way a nape turning away from me is a bride walking towards me, her hands veiled in a vermillion epic written with a crushed branch of henna *Yup, you'll find it right next to the coffee. Yup. Have a good one.* I am filing a petition for her eyes & her tendency to leave jars open, & the way a nape turning away from me is a bride walking towards me, her hands veiled in a vermillion epic written with a crushed branch of henna, its flowers kept aside, each of the four sepals pointing in one cardinal direction, the lobes spread thin & patient, each red stamen paired & perched, the petals ovate, & leaning across the cliff of night, into the gasp of the hungrier hours. During the third shift, you do not see her as I do, between the Haribo Gummies & the Sour Cream Ruffles: fluorescent, arms akimbo; sweet burrow, sweetest sparrow.

LAST PETITION

(or, USCIS FORM I-130 Spring Night Pastoral for Alien Relatives)

Ma, remember when we waded
into the form-field & pulled pussy willow
with inky palms, flicked buckeyes
into checklist boxes
swung on drop-down menus
like banyan branches, cut terraces
into the small print marshes, dragged
yoked highlighters through, roved through the footnotes
as you roamed unthreshed paddy,
& we— *yes, I remember, we*
parceled our family
into placeholders
that September,
& huddled in the warmth of an archive
set on fire.

This is what writing is: I one language, I another language, & between the two, the line that makes them vibrate; writing forms a passageway between two shores.

—Hélène Cixous, *Ladder Book*

LOCUTION / LOCATION

She sings the letters
to her great-granddaughter, strings them
marigolds into garlands
in the order of the alphabet
E, F, G, she
tugs the *haitch*, taut & long
far from the breast, a letter
the length of a coast, the width
of a gull's caw. She now carries
the *haitch* like I will carry the gurney
later, weightless
hammer
of feather
the letters swim with the orange petals
around & around her,
child & crone
milkflesh holme, mouthly
smelling of talc & gooseberry

When that song sills, will we
bury her in the sky
cirrus flight folded
into the pleats— riding the crest
& trench of her sari's
weave & weft?
Will we be left

with her
haitch
a patch of ash, just voiceless & glottal
an open casket fricative
an open hatch?

Haitch: listen, I am asking you for her
tongue, wrapped in twill
flung to its thatched edge; I am asking
for a body thrown so far
it meets itself
in the mouth. How do we bury her
haitch
one glyph on either side
arm in arm
*h*arm in *h*arm, how will we use this
twin ruddered
throat in an open boat
home?

H circles her tea, water sunk by cream,
A
B
C
D
E
F
G

haitch floats my grandmother's childbody, breastless
buoying, ankles cuffed in silver,
scales sequined on its heels
so it can stay, & stray, & swim with her
when she is restless, sugar hungry
when she is eighty & two hundred & twenty
heavy, human,
cane in fist, knife in hand
in the kitchen, thrumming
haitch, haitch, haitch
the percussive hinder, the fescues
of coriander, thunder
haitch, haitch, haitch
turns the lathe with each exhale
haitch, haitch, haitch
her belly, wet with sink & soap
its damp, equatorial girth
curls my mother
into her mother, hatchet
to hammock, split & swung
haitch, the waist in two
haitch, the lips in four
haitch, a longitude's wretch
I chart this stretch of tongue, I listen
for how her breath measures
the distance, pulls skin apart
to etch the gravity of gravidity

My daughter pouts yogurt out, plumbs
the berry, sun-smitten, filmed in milk, wades
her phonemic fen, hailing her elder, with bib & mitt.
But when this song sills, where shall we dig
us grandmotherless fools
us rudderless, us letterpoor
with drum & dread
where shall we dig
haitch, haitch, haitch
for this shibboleth of breath?

THRESHOLD

Sometimes the threshold is dressed in red dots, similar to the
red dot commonly seen on an Indian woman's forehead. The
dot is a symbol of the seed, the source of life
>   —Stella Kramrisch, qtd. in Vijaya Nagarajan,
>   *Feeding a Thousand Souls: Women, Ritual,*
>   *& Ecology in India – An Exploration of the Kōlam*

In the absence of reliable ghosts I made aria.
>   —Meena Alexander, "Birthplace with Buried Stones"

1.

I had been carrying her
six months. Within
me, she could open
her eyes, she could tell
dark apart from light. She could know
when daylight filtered
through the cathedral, a ray breaking
the sticky pane
cranberry stained
glass womb.

2.

When I read the news
of the shooting, this belly
plumed into an apse— it distended
upward, a balloon hollow
but leaden, these lungs lifted
here— this diaphragm fled, bore through
a tent made of ligament
& rope. The billow screeched
in these ears, pulled here— these legs apart
these toes went numb & cold. The ground
beneath me collapsed, turned to dunes
& the sand quickened. Here— this belly
carrying those pounds of flesh
began to take flight
in seconds it was

in— here— this mouth, pressing against here— these teeth—
a pear balloon, hot flush
with wet wings beating, with wet wings thrashing
in these lungs. The breath
an ocean of blood. This skin
here— a dam, detonating. A pulse, here
pulling history
towards these feet.

3.
When I read the news
of the shooting, I was standing
in our library & this— here— this face fell
into a hundred sheets
sheaves of visas lost in monsoon floods
a long queue dispersing after bad news
passes through breath & beard
a susurrus of shaking heads, shrugged shoulders;
this— here— this face fell
apart in the quiet hum of the air-conditioning
soft surplice, lisping off me, the bone simply giving way
the skin curling back, the cartilage of this nose spilling
a bib over this— here— pale nightshirt.
I needed this face
to stay; I wanted
this face to flee
to abandon me the way rats do ships
to stave off a starvation by drinking water

to make it to any shore, baby in mouth. I needed this
— here— face because it was on my visa.
I gathered it up— these knuckles
driftwood; these palms
sailcloth. These finger-tips
branched apart; each phalange dangled
— cheap pens at the mall's Western Union
chained & paranoid about being taken elsewhere.
The nails scratched the deck & that sound
drowned the sough of crowds
migrating within one.

4.

When I read the news
of the shooting, it was warm & bright outside
the cumin spun into rasam, the curds set just right.
I called my mother, it was dark & cold
where the news stained first, where the choke cleared
brushwood for a pyre
where she was. I called out
to my husband; I thought about my father
but I did not call him.

5.

When I read the news
of the shooting, the blowback
was a flight from the fear of ever seeing

a photograph
of my father's rib shattered, his blood
staining the pocket of his faded navy pique polo—
        the one he wears on Costco runs for bananas
        & two-packs of Windex.
was a flight towards the pale band of skin
on his wrist, where he keeps time—
        how he looks older, more lost
        when it isn't hidden by his watch—
I pocketed this band for the alms I would offer myself
        as I begged, in the months to come, for a place
        on a curb not wet with blood, of a question not always cocked
I remembered my father's future
as a passport-photo hung from an elm tree
as a headline
as a statistic gently rolling on a marquee.

That brown face, a stain
between kin & ken
between breech & brotherhood
on a floor near the boots
of citizens, Americans, men.

6.
When I read the news
of the shooting, these palms
began speckling; small white patches
bloomed & turned to face me

curds splotchy with pale pink mulberries
stamped & dragged, red & unripe, between skin
& muscle. This— here— body had crushed itself
while reading the news.
The she in me turned; faced herself. Cherry feet
fluttered at a sweetsop bladder; a migrant heartbeat
clattered like a clay pigeon.
The middle of the sky was pressed pause.

7.

When I read the news
of the shooting, these ears rang
the phone-lines of the dead, called
for the knowing trill, the scatter
of sugar, of a spoon circling
a milk tea for one
on the other side
of the world.

8.

When I read the news, the she in me
was swollen & pressing, & I saw
her dropping to kneel, her
brown belly
collapsed to a city's curb
her skull crimson in the clouds
her sweet ear flung & clinging

to a parapet. & at that cleft
for the first time, I saw
— here—
her as mine & then, hearing canons
sung in double-time
I knew being mine
would clip her life. So, I slipped
this burning hand
into a place
where this body hammers at its heart
& I singed its edges & with shame I
scorched a hole into the photograph
of an ancestor, blotted her dark
eyes out to whiteness, charred
her skin to a pale ash, turned
her folded hands into smoke, & I looked
within this— here— belly
for those eyes that could tell
dark apart from light, & I wished
out loud
so she could survive—

> *live*, I said,
> *in any skin, live.*

February 22, 2017. Srinivas Kuchibhotla was shot in a bar in Olathe, Kansas, by Adam Purinton, a white supremacist who believed that Kuchibhotla was an illegal immigrant from Iran. The shooter yelled, "Get out of my country!" before he shot & murdered Srinivas. Then, the shooter went to another local bar & bragged that he had shot an immigrant.

On that day, I was pregnant & moving into my third trimester.

MILESTONES:
A THEORY OF MARKING/ BEING MARKED

February. Winter, Michigan
(United States of America)
mishigamaa, large water

July. Monsoon, Tiruchirapalli
(India)
திருச்சிராப்பள்ளி, *three-headed,*
holy, rock town

Grey study. Laminated floor printed to look like a felled oak.

I squat in the direction of the West to face Lake Michigan.

The lake is a wet archipelago reaching into land, a beseeching arm. The lake is lined with fur, red & mottled, laden with grain, exchanged for a pelt, bought for a kettle, swapped for a gun, brindled by blood. This waterfront is wedged into the earth by a rock large enough to hold down a mastodon pierced by spear.

An absence forms around me, evacuates the room.

I squat to face Lake Michigan, move my arms to lap its water to my face. I squat in the direction of water brindled by blood & make myself into the shape of a milestone I have seen in my childhood— rough-hewn, curved at the head, jaunty, jammed into red laterite or crow black alluvial soil from the Kaveri delta.

The wedging body creates a space, insisting on mattering.

I lower myself to touch the floor, until my shins begin to strain
& my ass grazes the carpet's stylized oriental hyacinths (100%
acrylic); I bring to the hyacinth the partial shade of my thighs,
present to it the moisture of something spreading. I rise & turn
my body. Musk rises with me, & with it, a memory of the night.

I squat in the direction of South East to face the Kaveri delta,
a spreading flush nine thousand miles away. The delta is
placental, mother vein, rushing my ears, pulling me with her
into the Bay of Bengal. I bring my arms over my head, tuck my
chin in, draw my forehead in to face my heart. I listen for its
thrumming ventricle, its reddened kettle, whistling.

My breathing deepens. I am working for this breath. My face
prickles, turns numb, then stony. The blood leaving this place.
Leaving this place for elsewhere. On cars & planes, in boats
& trains.

The *Arthashastra* (370-250 BCE) states: "atoms (paramánavah)
are to be measured as one particle thrown off by the wheel of
a chariot." All matter consists of the fact of the journey & the
pressure exerted on this earth by a body in motion.

I rise & turn in the other direction.

A milestone is a stone propped beside a road to mark the distance to a particular place.

\\

It is matter. It was once pulled from a mountain or a quarry, mined & heaved & displaced, to mark the displacement of one body from point A to point B. It is a marker of movement, itself disoriented from an ancient context.

\\

Modern milestones are concrete slabs, like imposter headstones with numbers instead of names— 50, 60, 70. & in villages & towns where no stone can be drawn, they strip the bark off giant trees, & mark them with white paint— 50, 60, 70.

\\

A "milestone" in its idiomatic form isn't concerned with distance. Instead, it marks the movement of time & the development of a fleshthing growing into another fleshthing: the moment at which some infants can roll over onto their belly, the moment when some infants can pull themselves up by fingers curled around a bar, the moment when some children can walk backwards without keening over. It is a gong that sounds in families, a loud & insistent mark of movement, change, & some bodies normed & other bodies made inscrutable. One does not— cannot— make the journey back shadowed by the same milestones.

\\

A milestone presumes forward, onward; it presumes long
journeys; presumes the will of the animal that shall carry
you; presumes a machine that eats fuel milked from rock and
ancient rot.

\\

Passing milestones, a passenger looks forward along with
the driver of these animals, these machines. The passenger
is *agōnistés*, moving forward towards what they approach.
Their orientation is not concerned with memory, with what is
left behind.

Consider instead the cart drawn by oxen, where the passenger
sits facing backwards & away from the driver of the cart.
Antagōnistés: looking at the stretch of road left behind, the
landscape being dragged away from their faces, shoulders
shaking with the trot of hooves & the stagger of a bull's hump.

\\

In the ancient, undivided Indian subcontinent, mile pillars
marked roads approximately every 4000 yards— one for every
kos [कोस]; one red, phallic obelisk thrust to the sky, built with
brick & brushed with bright white lime.

A kos is an unfamiliar distance to bodies that move through Western spaces which are measured & weighed by the metric system, with its rounded edges & confident zeroes, with the certainty that arrives when one can divide anything in equal & even parts.

100 /10 =10.

One kos = the length of two thousand archers' bows [धनुष], twenty thousand human handspans [हाथ], ten thousand human forearms, forty thousand human fists with thumbs raised [धनुर्मुष्टि].

The kos measures distance with the body holding an archer's bow, with how far one needs to draw the bowstring, with a sense of when one needs to let go.

Distance is measured by a body & its analogy: a ranged weapon that functions through the tension between intent & aim, through a tension between drawing close & seeing far.

How do we measure the tension & displacement of a body in memories of having traversed, of having been moved, of having been so utterly moveable? What is the force that can lift a child into the air and throw her across the world?

\\

My father likes to say: *how far we have come*. My mother likes to say: *how long it has been*. I want a body that answers these questions together, knowing fully that these are not questions but statements about having arrived, somewhere, alone together.

\\

Every migrant body should keep company with its living milestones. To mark another day when it has roamed, without extinguishing itself in the fire of a crossing or being bludgeoned into forgetfulness or threatened into monolingualism.

Every migrant body should keep company with its living milestones— a witness held within the self— because so much of living is a kind of unmarked yet singular survival of the shame of having lived at all, of having crossed over, of having translated.

A mark in the body to remember the work of being discard.

A mark in the body to remember the work of being *itinerant-latecomer-belated-party crasher-imposter-undocumented-stranger danger-tresspasser-terrorist-gorgeous eyes-wherefromfrom-fresh off the boat-pretty hair-great asset-no offense takener-international talent-sorry to butcher your name-tax burden-welfare monster-visa monger-anchor babe-migrant-kith*.

A mark in the body to remember the work of being a paper person, with or without papers. A living milestone to mark the work of being nothing to you.

A mark in the body to remember the day when you leaned close to someone else who reminded you of someone you once held close. A stranger who is like family. Kith.

I keep a record of these milestones— selves garlanded to measure a distance. I make the marks. These are fleshy anniversaries of days on which I have not died; days on which I have agreed to be similar to someone; days on which I have yanked a flag planted in the earth & buried it; days I have consented to be kith for someone else; days on which I, for a brief, resplendent, filthy moment, remember who I am; days on which I have been moved by strangers who have moved me— knotted as we are to this route by hair & tooth, moving in a shared interior drawn taut across a map

& from that space of loneliness, I can feel the cab driver watching me in his rearview mirror. Be happy you can't read [white people's] thoughts, I want to say to him. I smile into the rearview mirror instead. Why with such a nice smile are you trying to weep? He asks as we pull up to my building.

—Claudia Rankine, *Don't Let Me Be Lonely*

MILESTONE 1
(WE SPEAK ABOUT YOUR DAUGHTER)

your uber has arrived
we ride
quiet, curious
there is an us
forming
a shoreline
serrates the seats
      his daughter— he says
      should marry, but his daughter— he says
      wants to study
      yes— I say
      she is right, as I was right
      & my father?— what does he do,
      does he live with me?
      no— I say
      I would like him to, but he
      must work— that is how it is for girls— he says
      & for us fathers— for us too, it is like this only

the traffic quivers an amber frill
on his brow. his mouth
parts, an oar catches
the water, drives
a stroke through silence

— for us too, for us too
    — for us too, for us too
        — for us too, for us too

what he wants to say
& cannot
is that my eyes
are the color
of shade, a dark
oval left on the earth
by a fig tree
from his hometown
seen in the rearview mirror
where I see: *us*
pulling into the East Village
next to an ailanthus tree
growing from a wall, its roots
a delta spreading
on red brick

MILESTONE 2
(WE LAUGH ABOUT THE WEATHER,
ITS PERMANENCE)

457 S Mariposa Ave
Los Angeles, CA

Head north on S Mariposa Ave toward W 4th St
0.2 miles

your uber has arrived
how are you today?
where are you from?

Turn left onto W 3rd St
0.6 miles

where are your parents from?
how many years have you lived here?
do you like it here?
are you able to bear the winters?
are they good to you at work?

Turn right onto S Western Ave
0.3 miles

do you go back often?
is your family here?
when will they come?
how does your wife like the movies here?
when will her papers be cleared?

Turn left onto W 1st St
0.3 miles

are your parents in good health?
how often do you see them?
do they like it there, without you?
where is your landlord from?

Turn left onto N Wilton Pl
0.7 miles

have the flights become more expensive?
when will the rains come this year?
will you be able to vote in that election?
when will the dam developers come?

when will your sister's wedding be?
will you be able to go for the wedding?
when will you see your children?
what is your daughter's name?
how often do you have to send money home?
when did they sell the buffalo?
how often can you send the insulin kits?
has the cost of onions gone up, again?
when did your father pass away?
when will they sell the farm?
how soon will the wells dry up?
when did your mother stop sleeping?

Turn left onto Melrose Ave 1st St
0.1 mile

Turn right onto N Van Ness Ave
0.1 mile

Destination will be on the right

MILESTONE 3
(WE ARE AT EASE IN OUR SILENCE)

your uber has arrived
I see your face & your first name
like my own & my last.
Sainted, coastal, Catholic.
I know our counterfeit halos, closed curves
twinned in a kind of black-market
trinity— Malabar, Coromandel, Konkan—
because we are *us us* even as we borrow
from the martyrs of Marseille, Damascus, Turin.
Our debts are to the banks
where we wash our children, where trespass
is unknown.

We recognize each other
from the self-published hagiographies,
the marginalia of visas & FAFSA forms
— the paperwork placed at altars & scented
with coconut & frankincense, syllables sooty
feathering the cathedral walls, each letter, oiled with the familiar
flinty viridescence of mackerel, apostolic & fluttering down
wiped with the edge of a lungi, the frayed plaid dotting
tea terraces warbling with a green
so wet it rivers my lap, so wet it migrates my throat
with psalms sung & palm arak drunk
near the glint of gold threads circling ankles in the silt.

These are the only orbits we've ever needed— അല്ലേ?
pelagic as we are, *us us,* & still twitching
in our skins kept on ice, still twitching to any shore that will have us,
to any shore with fin tagged, in pleated Dockers, armed to the gills
with a business degree framed & hung in the vernacular
of your amamma's veranda, washed green by moss & kept wet
by monsoon swash. Yet today, as we steer
the scorched tar along the Hudson
my slender question swims upstream
to meet your silence— how long, chetaa,
have we been here
before we arrived?

LAST MILESTONE
(WE LOOK OUT & UP AT THE SKY,
AWAY FROM THE ROAD)

your destination has arrived
I can barely hold
our privacies, upholstered
plush in the darkness
of this movement between us—
chaste
touching
borne by a chassis
of steel

There is no landscape that is not obscure, underneath its pleasing transparencies, if you speak to it endlessly.

—Édouard Glissant, *Philosophy of Relation*

Just got done walkin' in the snow / Goddamn, that motherfucker cold (cold, cold).

—Run the Jewels, *RTJ4*

LANDSCAPES (AS PORTRAITS):
OR THE POET AS CHILD-WITNESS TO U.S.
& INDIAN IMPERIAL EXPANSIONS (1990-1994)

As Operation Desert Storm erupted last week, there was only one unequivocal victor in the first days of war: The Cable News Network.

—*Variety Magazine*, January 20, 1990

[Maniratnam's *Roja*] perceives the [Kashmiri and Muslim] threat to the state as a threat to the Hindu-middle-class-nuclear-family.

—Venkatesh Chakravarthy and M. S. S. Pandian, *Economic and Political Weekly*, March 12, 1994

ARBOR/ ARDOR

for Mrigaa Sethi & Shivram Gopinath

We walk, a pair, past
eucalyptus trees. The sentries
flock off the peach in the sky, frame the street
smelling of crow shit. They dim the pink,
usher us to the open-air
theatre, where everywhere
this summer, they will screen
twelve rapes, one for each week
we are out of uniform, one
for each cheap peppermint, one
for each soda clear as rose water, dense as glass.

We walk, a pair, slip on socks,
fogged in red dust, orbiting
what was once stone, as dogs do dogs, hands the hips,
& we walk the anywhere walks;
our first *fuck-offs* slip out the edges
of our anywhere mouths
tasting flint & silt, tasting the selvage
between two girls sewn
into the landscape, spliced as we are
to cellulose, camphor, fiction,
strip over strip; we
rate ourselves: U— for Unrestricted Public Exhibition.

Our talk sprawls across the street.
We are drifting into dusk,
in skirts. A ruffle too close, a downy arm far, far too far,
past the single-serve-everythings, just-this-onces,
past the grotto frothing hibiscus over the Virgin's cape,
past velvet apostles, overdressed for this emergency,
each halo a hymen
between man & his god. We talk fast, fast too fast,
into each other, pull words like shell after wet shell
from the back-swash; we draw ourselves in our own image
in fast-forward, the silage of the ocean dragging itself back
from us *girls, girls, girls.*
We talk & we loiter all summer, annexed
into every garden we graze, called
rose, rose, rose,
clasp coins into purses, pocket all the curses
— one for each time we touch ourselves, for each time we speak
of how laps dissolve, how a scene cuts
how a mountain range marks the cusp
where one nation plunges
into another.

We just walk as girls do,
book-bags grinding into the small of our backs; we talk
to patch the shredded blouses, we caulk the gut tumult
in fear of salt or glance, we take it
in our stride, we count to twelve
for each time a sari is unreeled on screen
from an anchor, & beached near the navel
where the storyboard begins, pleats itself, then ends.

We saunter into the grass, cooling
the shape of us under a kite's scoot, we pierce
apertures into our anywhere feet, stud our knowing
to the law of sallow, count fireflies
soft soft   lit lit
envy their bellies blinking cold light, wait for ours to project
us us   us us

The projector beam, a stream of wan albumen, quivers all night.

We sit, letting history catch up,
but we have oiled our braids well, to slip
out of traps laid for us since we've known
that roads never go where roads claim to go,
since we've known how to hopscotch, how to follow the marled marble
          into mud, how to wait to cross over
until the hard-boiled sweet cracks
mid-sentence
like a frame, in two.

EN PLEIN AIR

If, on a day after the rains,
you go to the tamarind tree at the edge of the tar road,
you will find a man covered in chalk & white as fog,
sitting on the highest branch, courting crows, & cawing
to the clouds, & if you go the tamarind tree at the edge of the
    tar road,
& you find a man covered in chalk & white as fog,
sitting on the highest branch, courting crows, & cawing
to the clouds, on a day after the rains, & if he sees you
with his pumice eyes, & if he flaps you forward
with his flimflam arm, & if you, with your ink stained palms,
trip into the dust, & if you take off your sandals
& plop down your bag, & if you
look at the pocked dirt where the pods have dropped, & if you
pick up a smooth tamarind seed, hot & marooned
like a shear of liver from a lost body, & if you
slip it in your pocket, & if on a day after the rains,
this chalk man flops his limbs down
& they creep down the branches, & if you,
at the edge of the tar road, itch at your red feet & tug on a scab,
    & if,
when you aren't looking, the chalk man, on a day after the
    rains, in the whitest of quiet,
drops his limbs down, & creeps down the branches & pulls at
    your pinafore, & if you,
having walked off the tar road & into the dust,

having taken off your sandals & having plopped down your bag,
having looked away from the pocked dirt,
rubbing your ink-stained palms look straight at his milk-skin face,
when he, courting crows, & cawing
to the clouds, sees you with his pumice eyes, *then* you,
knowing how long your hands have been stained by ink,
    knowing how long you've expected
this man in the whitest of quiet, dig a well in the ground,
& you eke ink from the ground, & fill that well with ink,
&, then, you write:

> *On a day after the rains, when I went to the tamarind*
> *tree at the edge of the tar road, I found a man, covered*
> *in chalk & white as fog, sitting on the highest branch,*
> *courting crows, & cawing to the clouds & waiting*
> *for me, & I, having taken off my sandals, held him by*
> *his limbs of fog, pulled him from the highest branch,*
> *& drowned him in the well of ink that I dug with my*
> *small hands.*

GULF

Soak this; swell the gelatin
let me return to this scene
as often as necessary. I am back there
ogling a war which can't blink back.
There: me, uniform clad, book bagged,
biscuit handed, remote hungry
for an elsewhere war. For which a journalist
must have unspooled the films, dragged them
through a bath. A wake must have formed,
dovewet, parting the flesh, dividing the home
of a memory— having seen, having unseen.
That footage bloomed eyes
spacious as rooms scrubbed clean
of cells, of hair, of having roomed.

This is what the journalist gave me: America
rolling into a desert, wind peeling off
a peach skin, wet scab flagging;
the F-15 Eagles, cocked
& cradled (my rayon skirt
a bluster of dust, hands
scented rust red from swinging
on the swings, now held
to my mouth); a birthmark
descending the thighs in the shape of a nation
hatching itself in my lap;

the sights: a doorknob polished by use, a window
kissed by the fog of a mouth, her face
framed by the wreck; my own body
returned, used
as a measure for the depth of field.

In the racket of the rake, the cable company
ploughed our land, gave our sunflowers satellites,
made furrows for CNN. I am there
jamsandwiched, skorted, coiled into the shortbread gloat,
forgetful as hotels & cameras— as I am now,
watching reruns of this war, steeped in the sillage
of a stranger's shower, fretting a silken knot
of floss, annotating an aperture
sparked by scuds.

The architect's guide tells me
rubble is used to fill cavities
in buildings, where animals should not tread.
Ruins reamed from other ruins, stuffed
into the foundation. Let me return
to this scene, with an awful appetite
for that collapsible child,
made of clay & straw, once named
& made now of wattle & daub.
The thing pulled through
screens & aperçu, through
pebble & pumice, through
the line break

with skin glaucous as asphalt in the cross-hairs,
remote as a greenhouse, exposed.

In my draft now,
winter swelling at the sills, I return as a tourist,
airborne, draw an image from an archive of stone
in landscapes baffled by policy, seeded
for funeral flowers. Write:
she was strewn
rather than laid to rest.
All my poems are manifests
for burials elsewhere.
What good is an oeuvre
that does not include her?

If my memory is ashen, it is because
I have refused to Google *harm*.
Give me the names of the people
who have kissed her chin.
Let me write them letters
to say what this poem can't.

Stop bath & rinse,
then hang up this feeling
by its arms.

MORE CURBS

The city is an oeuvre, closer to a work of art than to a simple material product. If there is production of the city, & social relations in the city, it is a production & reproduction of human beings by human beings, rather than a production of objects.
—Henri Lefebvre, "The Specificity of the City"

CURB 1

you see the swelling
over here, yes, you see
the way the leg, yes?
yes, a long band, yes— that—
the horse's hock sunk, see
when you touch— that—
yes, feel the warmth?
trauma— see how his walk
is inflamed—
to the soft
tissues. see, it sets— yes? causes
differ: a sprain, stress,
race injury—
a gait
on fire

CURB 2

Mesa Star Chevron Gas Station
Mesa, Arizona

to bend	tall grasses
to edge	brittlebush
to bow	camphorweed
to restrain	pricklyleaf
to end	paperflowers

a knee   give way to yards folded

a handful   mulch red some selvage

a nod   hang flags then hang him

a sheaf   documented lullaby

& sign   here & here   & here

On September 15, four days after the attacks on the World Trade Center, Frank Roque told a waiter at Applebee's: "I'm going to go out & shoot some towelheads." He added: "We should kill their children, too, because they'll grow up to be like their parents." Roque murdered Balbir Singh Sodhi as he was planting flowers outside his own gas station.

CURB 3

Gold Coast Café
Hoboken, New Jersey

pushed   & pulled

an object described as a brick or a bat

toward   the building side

a path described as from a bar to a car

hit   a few times

a man described as bald

hitting   a fence

slumped

a sound made when a name falls from a face

to the ground

out of the center

of the sidewalk   *he* was

                                   he remembered

                                   & *he*
                                   to the ground

On September 27, 1987, Navroze Mody, a Zoroastrian, was
beaten with bricks and bats by eleven youths who were chanting
"Hindu! Hindu!" as he was walking out of the Gold Coast
Café with his friend William Crawford. Mody died in hospital,
four days later, of trauma to the brain. The assault is often
cited in reports about a cluster of incidents perpetrated by the
hate-group Dotbusters, who specifically targeted any "Patel" or
anyone wearing a dot on their forehead.

CURB 4

Subway Station
Queens, New York

of gray   concrete

                           son

of gray   asphalt

                           traveler

of gray   wool

                           quiet

of gray   grisaille

                           after drinks

of gray   charcoal

▮▮▮▮▮▮   a pigment

rain damp	battleship water	
print-shop owner	*roommate*	grey
smoking bitumen	wolf fur	
entrepreneur	*immigrant*	grey
undyed robes	bristle collar	
"an Indian Gregory Peck"	*nice*	grey
still, wet frescoes	flesh of flesh	
after breakfast	*after dinner*	grey
animal bones	white lead	
		grey
an immediate	in between	

On December 27, 2012, Sunando Sen, a print-shop owner &
immigrant who had lived in the United States for 16 years,
was pushed off the subway platform & onto the tracks of an
oncoming 11-car No.7 train by Erika Menendez. After her
arrest, she told the police: "I pushed a Muslim off the train
tracks because I hate Hindus & Muslims ... ever since 2001
when they put down the twin towers I've been beating them up."

CURB 5

High School Football Field
Lawrence Township, New Jersey

To the brown boys
on the bleachers
shaking their fists
at the black girls
on the turf,
& the brown boys
on the bleachers
pointing their fingers
at the black girls
on the turf,
& the brown boys
on the bleachers
climbing over each other to hurt
the black girls
on the turf,
& the brown boys
on the bleachers
breaking their throats, screaming death
at the black girls
on the turf:
The same sun that darkens our skin
bleaches the cheap boards
you stand on. You: a lackey

to supremacy, feeling free
winning when you're
bootlicking. We
want to know:

        Who taught you, brothers,
        to want whiteness for your kin?
        Who taught you, brothers,
        to hate the dark flesh
        that you're in?

                1. _____
                2. _____
                3. _____
                4. _____
                5. _____

In October, 2019, at a sporting event, two 17 year old high school students of Indian descent perched on bleachers menaced four black students, their peers, by screaming racial epithets and verbally threatening their lives. The young men of Indian descent were performing a familiar policing of space and black bodies. They were establishing their own roles as agents of white supremacy by producing anti-blackness. They were, as Nell Irvin Painter has argued, extending what sociologist Elijah Anderson calls "the white space" even though the spaces in question are officially public." When South Asians perform anti-blackness as a form of a centuries-long aspiration to be white, we erase and destroy an equally long history of coalition between black and brown folk, and fail to acknowledge our debt to civil rights processes that have guaranteed the relative freedom of Desis in the United States.

CURB 6

Bedrooms & Bathrooms & Altars in the Diaspora

CHOOSE YOUR DESIRED CURB:

☐ **INDO-ARYAN STOCK**
e.g. like Mohandas Karamchand Gandhi's racist claim that
he should be categorized as white in his protest against
being labeled with an "N" (for [black] "Native") in the
South African prison system, so as to be distinguished from
those he labeled
"k_ _ _ _ _s" and described as savage, indolent, raw.

Indian Opinion, 1908

☐ **DESCENDENT OF ARYANS OF INDIA (BUT BRUNETTE)**
e.g. like Bhagat Singh Thind, who claimed that he should
be allowed citizenship in the United States because he was a
High Caste Brahmin who was a "descendent of the Aryans
of India." The Courts ruled that "the words 'white person'
are words of common speech and not of scientific origin"
and so determined that Thind was indeed "Too Brunette to
Vote Here."

The Literary Digest, March 10, 1923

☐ BASICALLY CAUCASIAN

e.g. like Sakharam Ganesh Pandit, who was accorded citizenship in the United States of America because the Judge held that Pandit is "of a Caucasian race from an ancient Indo branch," who then made a living by being a "High Caste Brahmin Teacher and Lecturer from India" and by peddling casteism and Brahmanical superiority on the Wisconsin Dells Chautauqua Circuits in the 1900-1910s.

☐ FAIR & LOVELY

e.g. like Priyanka Chopra endorsing POND'S "White Beauty" cream "which gives you a pinkish white glow."
e.g. like literally every one of *The Mindy Project*'s love interests.

☐ NEELI AANKHEN / GORE GAAL

e.g. like the TOP HITS from *Chitchor* to *Baazigar* to Yo Yo Honey Singh to *Chennai Express*, feat. that cool blend of misogyny and timeless colorism.

☐ WHEATISH

i.e. like Shaadi.com and BharatMatrimony.com slush piles
i.e. like get out of the sun, or you'll get too dark to marry, besharam, chi!

CURB 7

a western bridle
has a curb chain or
a curb shank or
it is a strap or
it is a piece of leather or
it buckles
to each side
of your face &
if you pick up
near the mouth
you'll notice
that it hits
right at the bottom
of your chin.

& our parents began to fear for our lives whenever we walked out the door/ Because they read the news.

—Heems, "Patriot Act" *Eat Pray Thug*

PAVEMENT

Residential Neighborhood
Old Bridge, New Jersey

I forget the *his* name walking up the stairs
all the fricatives abandoned in the basement
where I read the *his* news reports— early casualties

at the foot of the *my* desk. these dog eared returns
never lead me to him *you* only
to myself य & your *his* own name interrupts   here
mine *his* scatters *jə* in the sugar bowl

                                        just minutes
after I learn it— my mouth tangles the *their* ligatures
saṃyuktākṣara the *his* ligaments between consonants
swung vines sung twine around the *my* teeth

                              व   य

snap

                              və   *j*

of a *schwa*
a blood line
ə

                              व्य

ः

a vowel's attachment to a consonant is inherent
a virāma is a diacritic mark that cancels

this attachment
end, cease
⁚

a consonant represented without
a vowel is known as a dead consonant

in the courtroom
your *the* wife says "their father"
the friction of breath, the how of air from *the* her

                                                        there

rubbing against an *f* or a *th*
whose father's body did they
he & *he* & *he* plunder

                                                        "wilding ride"

on the curb
who combed *the* your black hair matted
by blood & parted at *the* his color line
when she says your name *the* her shoulders are perched   a stone edge
the her voice lofted *the* her head lowered
she refers: *the* her index finger underlines the letters   on a bit of loam
fins glide in pooling ink   yards away
a childhood habit of tracking the traffic of glyphs   fist into face
across oceans   sinks

what did they call you?
when did you stop answering—
there

far is a place
a place farthest from home

In June 2010, Divyendu Sinha was assaulted in Old Bridge, New Jersey, mere yards away from his suburban home. He was taking an after dinner walk with his wife, Alka, & his two sons, Ashish & Ravi, when a car-load of assailants— on a spree— beat him into a coma. Sinha died shortly after. Sinha's work in New Jersey was concerned with life-support technologies.

FREQUENCY (ALKA'S TESTIMONY)

for Serena Chopra

1

the rate at which something occurs or is repeated over a particular period of time

2

the rate at which a vibration occurs that constitutes a wave, either in a material (as in sound waves), or in an electromagnetic field (as in radio waves & light)

Originally denoting a gathering of people: from Latin *frequentia*— "crowded, frequent."

Three years after the death of her husband Divyendu Sinha, Alka Sinha appeared at a Courthouse in New Brunswick to offer testimony in response to the Court's sentencing of the men who were responsible for his death. She began her testimony by playing a recording of Divyendu's voice-mail greeting. She closed it by walking away from the podium. His recorded voice & her living voice were buried together in a soundscape of this courtroom. The duration of her entire testimony, documented in these ten sequences, was eight minutes.

>>Honorable Judge I will like to play a an audio um recording for of the my husband's voice. Can I have that?

>>I'm sorry, Ma'am?

>>I will like to play a video recording a audio recording

>>OK

SEQUENCE 1

f   The hollow, wind-blown plunge of dry bamboo /or a
         pair of pencils shifting in a circular tube

f   The breathy fret of ten or fewer sheets of heavy duty
         cardstock or one sheet of vinyl being moved a short
         distance in a vertical, swift act /or a camera shutter

f   A distant click of a camera shutter /or the snap of thin
         plastic (from left of witness)

f   The soft lift of plastic, followed by a sharp click of
         plastic, followed by deeper thud of plastic against wood
         or wood-like material (such as Formica)

f   A series of stuttering shutter snaps in quick succession /
         or a rash of plastic scraping plastic

SEQUENCE 2

f   A lean breath taken in sharply through the nose, in
        preparation for an utterance or to clear an irritation

f   The drone of static in a recording prior to the presence
        of a human voice

f   The hum enveloping the flesh of a human voice
        recording

SEQUENCE 3

f   The lift & drop or flip of a piece of paper, shuffled / or a piece of paper hitting another piece of paper equally thin

f   A sharp & thick click of plastic (such as a switch)

f   The velvety hiss of the shift & lift & of paper against wood or wood-like material (such as a table or a clip-board)

f   A lightweight material placed or removed (to be replaced) with a quick act onto wood or wood-like material (behind witness)

f   A lightweight metal clip or fastening being moved across paper & hitting, lightly, a table or podium

SEQUENCE 4

f   The click of ballpoint or gel pen (in front of witness)

f   The quick scatter of flatness because of a flip or thumbing of a small stack of copy-grade paper

f   The fuller flipping of paper (on to the other side)

f   The click of a ballpoint or gel pen (in front of the witness)

f   The finite pat of placing a flat, narrow, light, small object on to a desk or table

f   The bone-snap or knuckle-crack quick & blunt sound of a thin stack of papers folded at the midriff

f   The scrape of a taping knife against a wall /or a page turning back & forth & back again like the sound of a double take

SEQUENCE 5

f   A hollow, sharp, & bent note of feedback from a
distant source (above witness)

f   A distant click (from left of witness) of camera shutter
or snap of thin plastic

f   The wispy slide of two or three fingers over a page

f   The flipping or counting of a series of thin sheets of
paper folded towards each other in a deliberate, slow
succession (to left of witness)

f   A cluster of thin & metallic crumpling sounds— a cold
or crisp page being turned, lifting into still air & then
settling on a podium (stapled stacks in humid rooms
clatter less)

SEQUENCE 6

f   A very sharp, wet intake of breath through the nose to
suggest the retention of thin mucous

f   A quick lap of a lush ripple— a slower turn or flip of a
crisp page (to left of witness)

SEQUENCE 7

f   A sharp, hard-edged shift or bending of paper

f   A series of uneven cracking of something flimsy (front & right of witness)

f   A louder drop of a stack of papers (from a short distance)

f   The tap of something metallic but light being placed down (like a demitasse spoon)

f   The fuller flipping of paper (on to the other side)

SEQUENCE 8

f   A quick & punchy gathering of stapling sounds/or a camera shutter

f   A series of quick & punchy sounds like a stapler/or camera shutter

f   A thicker, more robust turn or flip of a page

f   The short rattle of wooden beads or garland of dried flowers (behind witness)

f   A gauzy haze of paper separated from paper, as if laid out side by side

f   The flutter of three or fewer pages near hands or something soft

SEQUENCE 9

f   The creaking of something small & wound tight
(behind & to right of witness)

f   A sharp click of a turned page

f   The smack of a clutch of very thin sticks against
something plastic /or a camera shutter

SEQUENCE 10

f   The wobble or wah-wah of feedback (above witness)

f   A soft intake of breath or sniff to retain thin mucous

f   A slick smack from a thicker clutch of very thin sticks
or a camera shutter

f   Something slippery but light being gathered up (like
sheets of ice) very close to witness

ESTATES:

LAST OFFICES CONCERNING THE CURBS
OF THE BODY

THE EYELIDS

pass a warm
palm over *him* thin
skin to fold over
seeing, being seen
rows of lashes
mark margins
that blink to keep
out foreign bodies
⏝ hung हम
eaves curb a
vowel, clip a
stretch of breath
/brev/, to
grieve *he*

THE JAWS

place a pillow
& prop it shut
stop collapse
& plunder from
the gaping
vault, bar
the unmarked /greɪv/.
  ↘ , hoist
  ↗ , dig
how tall a vowel *he*
towers, where the tongue
is raised to the roof
or a torch to a tomb; how
quickly *his* lungs fill
with dirt when we found
him roving for a bed
beyond the sea
— विदेशी

THE BLADDER

press *him* down
collapse the billow
tent, sea-large
sac, push soft
until the day drains
until thirst
hooks under fugues
dries the sibilance
from *her* widowed tongue.
   ❩ , parch
with ash & milk
& lull a head below
the apse *her* दुपट्टा
voiceless at this cedilla
& wait. *Her*
सांस senses another
bony ridge, parts
state from state
matter from mattering

THE ANKLE

:
two dots
descend
a vertical line,
equal & swung
one
under
one
offers
an explanation, or
evidence for a claim, or
a list, or
two dots
narrate a ratio, tell how
many of one thing here
is for another thing there,
or it follows the
name of the patient: Indian American Techie mistaken for
                           Indian Engineer at Bar mistaken for
                           Alleged Hate Crime Victim mistaken for
                           Austin's Shooting Victim mistaken for
                           Indian Tech Worker mistaken for
                           Iranian mistaken for
                           Illegal Immigrant mistaken for
                           Indian mistaken for Patel mistaken for
                           Man mistaken for Executive mistaken for

Arab mistaken for Towel-head mistaken for
Hindoo mistaken for Muslim mistaken for
Terrorist mistaken for Rich mistaken for
Thief mistaken for here mistaken & taken,

or it follows the
date & time of death: when three men & a baseball bat; when
a dozen youths & bricks & fists; when
one man & a car & a gun; when five
men & a car & a knife,

or it follows the
patient ID number: the first son; the second born; the third
to migrate; the fourth to buy a house;
the fifth to go to college; the sixth to
hit the wicket; the seventh to pluck the
still-raw gooseberries; the eighth to
drop the baseball; the ninth to crease
the bag of chips; the tenth to fall back
asleep; the eleventh to plant tomatoes
in January; the twelfth tallest in sixth
grade; the thirteenth in the line for a
chocolate glazed; the fourteenth tooth,
& the day it pushed out; the fifteenth
page; the sixteenth kiss; the seventeenth
wick lit under your photograph; the
eighteenth marble pocketed, slick
with summer sweat; the nineteenth
cardamom seed floating in the tea;
the twentieth run on your own turf;

                              the twenty first day, when your body is
                              sent home,
or it follows the
name of ward: we've been making room for bones on
                              the streets where we hotdog hopscotch
                              drop hot on pavement for so long
                              since rubber ran its milk down our
                              bark is soft our bite softer we've been
                              making room for snow spray where the
                              tar steams where our limbs loll, or it
                              follows one dot below another dot,
a pinch of vermillion lifted to a face
a forehead aflame
with ghosts
because we occur
in pairs
one
after
another
for safety & not to enumerate
or demonstrate a relation
but
our apposition is mistaken for opposition:
                                        a dot
                                        is pressed
                                        one
                                        above
                                        another

:
& is written
on a scrap tied to a place
which holds your feet
to the ground.

NOTES & OBJECTS CITED

the yearning to begin again together
animals ken inside the parliament of the world

the people in the room the people in the street the people

hold everything dear
> —Gareth Evans "Hold Everything Dear
> (For John Berger)," 2005

Citation is how we acknowledge our debt to those who
came before; those who helped us find our way when the way
was obscured because we deviated from the paths we were
told to follow.
> —Sara Ahmed, *Living a Feminist Life*, 2017

SETTLEMENT

1. This poem was first drafted as an occasional piece to document my fear and reluctance in attending an all-white Thanksgiving dinner with my husband's family on land traditionally and contemporarily occupied by Odawa, Potawatomi, and Peoria peoples. The poem ends with the hearkening of a wishbone drawn from the clavicle of a bird whose life has been prepared for consumption. The chief function of this forked bone is to strengthen the chest against the force and friction of flight. Western Medieval practices used a goose's wishbone to divine weather for travel and trade. Teutonic knights used it to divine war strategy. My grandfather Ralph Simon used it to amuse his little daughter, my mother, who was the first to show me how a brittle and forked path made of bone could be pulled apart by two people fighting for only one wish to come true.

2. DMS Coordinates. DMS = Degree. Minute. Second.
   e.g. 40°41'58" N (Latitude) / 74°02'30" W (Longitude) are the DMS coordinates for Ellis Island, the United States' first immigration inspection center. It was in operation from 1992 to 1954 before it was incorporated into the tourist destination now called (Statue of) Liberty.

A reader might find the location of any of the marked poems in *Curb* using the facility at www.gps-coordinates.net.

The practice of marking the corners of pages with DMS coordinates initiates a conversation between the conceptual-visual practice in Erica Baum's *Dogear* (2011), which theorizes reading as a kinesthetic and volitional act that leaves traces, and the life-work of Srinivas Kuchibhotla, who was an Indian aviation systems engineer at the GPS manufacturer Garmin when he was murdered by white supremacist and nationalist Adam Purinton in Kansas. Baum writes: "Along with marginalia, underlining, and other notational strategies, dog ears map a history of reading and remind us that reading is a physical act… A dog ear is legible as a readerly engagement with the material text. Someone read *this*; someone stopped *here*." Before he opened fire, Purinton yelled "Get out of my country!" having misread Srinivas for an undocumented Iranian. Purinton imagined the United States as a location that should not be marked by the presence of immigrants, with fatal consequences.

Erica Baum, "Photographs from *Dog Ear*," *Jacket2*. March 9, 2011

SINCE YOU ASKED

This poem was written for the occasion of my first public walk with my mother after I returned (from Singapore) to a United States newly governed by Donald Trump's administration in September of 2017. Her confession became the threshold I would cross in order to enter the making of this book. A birth-pang. Tamilians cross the thresholds of homes with the right foot, followed by the left (in the opposite direction of written Latin script).

1. "in the land of the free / & the home of the brave" quotes the US national anthem "The Star-Spangled Banner," which uses the language from a poem written by Francis Scott Key in 1814.

HEDGES

1. The word "patient" comes from Middle English < from Old French < Latin *patiens*- "suffering", from the verb *patiors*- "I am suffering."

2. Indigo is a color named from the Latin word for "Indian" because the dye was exported from India to Europe through the Silk Road. The traditional Cherokee method of extracting plant indigoes is documented as follows:

> "We raised our indigo which we cut in the morning while the dew was still on it; then we put it in a tub and soaked it overnight, and the next day we foamed it up by beating it with a gourd. We let it stand overnight again, and the next day rubbed tallow on our hands to kill the foam."

Knight, Oliver (1956–57), "History of the Cherokees, 1830–1846," *Chronicles of Oklahoma*, Oklahoma City: Oklahoma Historical Society, p. 164

3. The indigo bunting, a blue passerine bird, migrates at night using the stars to chart its path. In captivity, the bird suffers disorientation because it cannot see the stars from its cage.

"All About Birds." *Cornell Lab of Ornithology*. 2003.

4. FS-240 and DS-1350 are US immigration and travel forms that offer a "Consular Report of Birth Abroad" to certify that a child has acquired U.S. citizenship at birth (if birthed in a foreign nation).

5. "aari ro ari   raro [...]" transliterates a well-known Tamil lullaby or தாலாட்டு (thaalaatu), literally "tongue rhythm" or "tongue rocking." In this poem, I am quoting a song from the Tamil film *Panchavarna Kili (Macaw)* (1965), written by Bharathidasan and Vaali.

6. "ज़मीन." Zameen, Urdu and Hindi. Literally "ground" or "land." This is also the name of our child.

7. ذِکْر. Dhikr or Zikr, Arabic. Recitation of rhythmic arrangements of the names of God as a devotional practice, particularly in but not limited to Sufism. Prayer beads are often used as a way of keeping track of counting and uttering the names for the Divine.

8. "ex ovum pluribus." Latin. Literally "Of many, egg," which detourns "e pluribus unum" ("Of many, one"), the motto of the United States, which appears on documents impressed with the Great Seal of the nation.

LAWN (TEMPERATE)

1. "two Bills." In the first section of Bernadette Mayer's *Midwinter Day* she recounts seeing two Bills in a dream, and this event becomes one in a series of dream-encounters during which some people become substitutes for other people.

LAWN (ARID)

1. This poem catalogues a variety of ecological traces in a memory of Trichy, India.

Dust/ Red dirt at dusk: Red loam, when dry, weathers easily because of wind movement. It will leave a trace on standing vehicles, hanging clothes, and very still children. Cleaning red dust off my clothes before entering sites of reading and recitation (at school or at music lessons) became for me a ritual practice of acknowledging the land resting on the body.

Cows: Konganadu cows are indigenous to Erode and Coimbatore. Umbalcherry cows are native to Thanjavur. The bob and quaver of the bullock's hump is one of the earliest registers of rhythm in my memory.

Snail trail. The African Giant snail which crawled all over my childhood was introduced to India in 1847, a century before the country's independence. William Henry Benson had given a pair to his neighbor before leaving Calcutta— a slippery symbol of shelter always carried on the back of an invasive species.

Weed & bramble: *Cyperus rotundus*. In Ayurvedic practice, this is consumed for fevers and the pain of blood pulsing out of the uterus. *Amaranthus viridis*: Also called callaloo in Jamaica, or kuppacheera in Kerala (literally, "rubbish spinach").

Badminton: Or, shuttlecock. The shuttling cock, introduced into modernist poetics by Mina Loy in *Songs to Johannes*: "shuttle-cock and battle-dore / a little pink love / And feathers are strewn" is a high-drag feathered missile also called a "birdie" and is made by overlaying sixteen duck feathers and pinning them into a cork (*Last Lunar Baedecker*, 56). The shuttlecock was my first memory of a decontextualized bird— a feather plucked out of its original context, and thus a citation flying in the air.

Marigolds: These are universally used all over South Asia, in garlands or in piles or as bright ochre heads floating in water. They bloom at funerals, births, weddings, and religious rituals. I enjoy eating the petals. After indigo, marigold orange is the color most likely to bring me to my knees.

Marianne De Nazareth, "Sluggish Invaders," *The Hindu*, Bengaluru. Oct 12, 2015.

Palanisamy Priyadharsini & Dharmadurai Dhanasekaran, "Diversity of soil Allelopathic Actinobacteria in Tiruchirappalli district, Tamilnadu, India." *Journal of the Saudi Society of Agricultural Sciences.* Vol. 14, Issue 1, January 2015.

BEDS (CLAY)

1. "sioux quartz." This pink, dusty quartzite is formed by braided river deposits in the Midwest of the United States, particularly in Indiana, South Dakota, Minnesota, and Michigan. Plains Indians used kalinite from this quartz to make pipes. Chips from this quartz lines gardens around Michigan. They are harvested from exposed outcrops that would have been submerged by ancient seas that covered most of the continent, from the Gulf of Mexico to Canada. The theory of the "Western Interior Seaway" suggests that we stand on land that was once water. It is always possible to drown a boundary or break a wall with a wave.

"Precambrian Sioux Quartzite at Gitchie Manitou State Preserve, Iowa." *Centennial Field Guide Volume 3: North-Central Section of the Geological Society of America:* Vol. 3, No. 0 pp. 77–80. 1987.

2. "purple sunbirds." Purple-rumped sunbirds (*Leptocoma zeylonica*) are indigenous to southern India and Sri Lanka. They know how to make a nest anywhere from a bit of cobweb, a fan of leaves, and a pinch of lichen.

Rahul Bagal, "Purple-Rumped Sunbird." India-Birds.com

BLOOD/ SOIL

1. The poem's title references the German slogan "Blut und Bloden" which was used as a rallying cry for Nazi Germany's eugenicists, nationalists, and racists. This anti-Semitic and anti-migrant slogan had the specific function of reifying the notion of a pure, agricultural, pre-industrial Germany. In 2017, white nationalist and supremacist protesters in the U.S. chanted this slogan during the gatherings (called the "Unite the Right rally") at Emancipation Park in Charlottesville, Virginia.

Meg Wagner, "Blood and soil:' Protesters chant Nazi slogan in Charlottesville." *CNN*. August 12, 2017.

2. The poem owes a debt to information from the following sources:

Andy Campbell, "Judge Throws Out Excessive Force Case Against Officer Who Injured Indian Man." *Huffington Post Politics*. Jan 10, 2017.

Challen Stephens, "Indian grandfather faces long recovery after police takedown, wants to know 'why?'" AL.com (no date).

Maureen Friedman, "'It was devastating:' a family struggles to recover from brutal Alabama beating." *The Guardian*. Feb 16, 2015.

3. "I slouch to the writing sideways" and "stony sleep" are references to W.B. Yeats' "The Second Coming." *The Collected Poems of W. B. Yeats* (1989).

4. "The Law says." Isaac Newton's Laws of Motion are the foundation of our current understanding of mechanics. They were first published

in his *Philosophiæ Naturalis Principia Mathematica (Mathematical Principles of Natural Philosophy)* (1687).

5. "camphorweed." A close-reading of the BBC video report on Sureshbhai Patel's case shows yellow-headed weeds in bloom at the site of the violent assault. The weed is perennial, fragrant, hairy, and bristly to touch. I owe a debt to environmental scientist Dr. Jaime Jo Coon (Earlham College) for helping me identify this plant.

PETITIONS (FOR AN ALIEN RELATIVE)

1. Much of the content for this poem is inspired by the bureaucratic language of Form I-130 (Petition for an Alien Relative), which is published by the United States Citizenship and Immigration Services (USCIS).

2. "Can you name two national U.S. holidays?" and "Who lived in America before the Europeans arrived?" are versions of questions that are a part of the "Civics (History and Government) Questions for Naturalization Test."

3. "batter sours too late." A culinary concern for Tamilian immigrants in general, and wives, in particular, when they work and live in the colder parts of the United States. Dosai batter, made from ground-up urad lentils and raw rice, is sometimes left in an oven with the light on, all night, to re-create the conditions of a humid, summer night in India. In a darkened house, the warm glow of an oven holding fermenting batter is like a lamp left burning to show a traveler her way home.

4. "dotterels." The Eurasian Dotterel male incubates and rears the chicks while the female travels to find more mates and resources. This is an inversion of migration and conventional domestic arrangements in South Asian families, where newly married couples spend long periods alienated from each other because of racist and uneven immigration policies, placing disproportionate social burdens on partners of temporary workers and immigrants or newly naturalized citizens in the United States.

5. "IMF." Several studies have shown that the leading cause of social crises, particularly suicides among rural farmers, has been caused by market reforms led by the IMF and the World Bank, which seek to impose western free-trade policies in decolonizing nations. Vandana Shiva, in particular, has done important work to highlight the plight of farmers caused by engagements with giant seed conglomerates (like Monsanto) and market liberalization pressures.

6. "terrapin." The Indian pond terrapin is classified as "near threatened." As omnivores, they will arrange themselves in a circle around a carcass to consume death.

7. "sugarcane." South Asian markets for sweeteners shifted from jaggery (gur) to sugar in response to colonial pressures produced by the Portuguese occupation of Brazil, the British occupation of the Caribbean, and the Dutch occupation of Java (now Indonesia). The abolition of Britain's trade of enslaved people in the 1830s resulted in the market bucking in ways that jostled and displaced millions of South Asian sugar laborers, who had to begin making a living in new corners of various empires. The systems of agricultural debt maintained under neo-colonial conditions now crushes sugar farmers in the mills of modern-day inequities produced by a global penchant for refined sweetness.

8. "laughing doves." A common motif in South Asian block printing and textile traditions. Along with stylized images of flowers, gods, camels, peacocks, and fruit, these birds become part of a visual taxonomy worn on the body. One could walk through a crowd at a protest or a public prayer in the diaspora and spot a bevy of printed doves around someone's hips or lined up against their chest like a feathered sash. We decorate our bodies with animals and birds to make artful a resemblance that we can barely articulate.

9. "Haribo gummies." These tiny, sweet, supple bears are made from the skins of pigs stripped for their collagen, which is the substance that stops your face from cracking when it opens itself to smile.

LOCUTION / LOCATION

1. "H." The pronunciation of the letter "H" differs based on national, class, and educational background. Jo Kim of the BBC's "Pronunciation Unit" suggests that our views on received pronunciation have shifted and globalized. While so-called Queen's English and British dictionaries would have us say 'aytch" as the standard pronunciation, "*haytch* is also attested as a legitimate variant."

2. "shibboleths" are customs and practices that distinguish one group of people from another. Within language practices, this distinction extends to pronunciation, accent, and stress, which are all markers of belonging and unbelonging. Pronunciation is risk. The pronunciation of "Brot and Cawse" for "Bread and Cheese:" This marked the Flemish and Dutch strangers during the English peasant rebellion (1380s). The pronunciation of the Spanish word for "parsley": This marked the Haitians living in Spanish dominant Dominican Republic under the dictatorship of Rafael Trujillo.

Holding up a sprig, a soldier would ask: *"¿Cómo se llama esto?"* The Creole tongue of a Haitian would fold out the flat R instead of rolling out a trilled R— her road to freedom from genocide. These are the consonant consonants; the vowels of vulning. For some, opening the mouth to simply say "I" also means saying "Aye," assenting to certain fates. Our methods for taming the tongue have grown more sophisticated— it no longer lolls out like some crude imperial leash— and yet, hundreds of thousands of South and Southeast Asians today undergo accent neutralization as part of the service industry's commitment to providing monolingual Americans with an emotionally secure and trustworthy consumer experience.

David Sillito, "'Haitch' or 'aitch'? How do you pronounce 'H'?" BBC News Magazine. 28 October 2010.

Caroline Bergvall and Ciarán Maher *Say: "Parsley"* (Liverpool Biennial, 2004).

Tim McNamara and Carsten Roever, *Language Testing: The Social Dimension* (Oxford: Blackwell Publishing, 2006).

THRESHOLD

1. The name "Srinivas" refers to Lord Venkateswara, the "destroyer of sins." Hindus believe that this divine force takes the form of a dark-faced deity with four arms, standing on a bed of lotuses, carrying a wheel and a conch shell.

2. In an interview with the *New York Times*, Sunayana Dumala, Srinivas Kuchibhotla's widow, stated: "My story needs to be spread...Srinu's story needs to be known. We have to do something to reduce the hate

crimes. Even if we can save one other person, I think that would give peace to Srinu and give me the satisfaction that his sacrifice did not go in vain." Srinivas' mother, speaking to reporters at his funeral in Hyderabad, said: "My son had gone there [to the US] in search of a better future. What crime did he commit?"

3. The FBI's statistical findings on hate crimes for the year 2017 are as follows: "Hate crimes towards Sikhs in the U.S. tripled from 20 incidents in 2017 to 60 incidents in 2018; There were 82 Anti-Arab hate crimes recorded in 2018— the second-highest total since the FBI added an anti-Arab category in 2015; There were 188 anti-Muslim hate crimes recorded, down slightly from last year but the fifth-highest total on record; There were 14 anti-Hindu hate crimes recorded in 2018— down from 15 in 2017; of the known offenders, over 50% identified as white."

4. Adam Purinton, who murdered Srinivas Kuchibhotla and shot Alok Madasani and Ian Grillot (a white American who intervened) in Olathe (Kansas), misrecognized the Indian men as Iranians, presuming them to be living in the United States illegally and (implicitly) as Muslims. The hate-crime is evidence not only of anti-immigrant sentiment but also of Islamophobia, which both impacts and *implicates* South Asian (specifically Indian) communities in the Unites States, where so-called "high-caste" Hindus have attempted to bolster their hold on various vectors of power through the perpetration of Brahmanical patriarchy and supremacy.

5. The poem owes a debt to information from the following sources:

Audra D. S. Burch, "He Became a Hate Crime Victim. She Became a Widow." *New York Times*. July 8 2017.

Lauren Smiley, "After Srinivas Kuchibhotla's Murder, His Widow Fights for Her Home: How one tech worker's story illuminates the plight of H-1B holders." *Wired Magazine*. August 22, 2017.

SAALT's aggregate release, "FBI Releases 2018 Hate Crimes Report: Hate in the U.S. is getting deadlier." November 12, 2019.

MILESTONES: A THEORY OF MARKING/BEING MARKED

1. Much of this section owes a debt to ideas contained in *The Arthashastra*, a 2nd or 3rd Century treatise on statecraft and economics, ethics and civil policies, traditionally ascribed to Chanakya (Kautilya).

MILESTONE 1-4

2. The reference to the Ailanthus tree owes to the letters contained in *The Horticulturist & Journal of Rural Art & Rural Taste* (1852), which documents the (white) nationalist advocacy to remove certain species of plants and trees from cities that were hubs of diversifying demographics and which, in particular, became symbols for anxieties around immigration: "We confess openly that our crowning objection to [the Ailanthus tree], this petted Chinaman or Tartar, who has played us so falsely, is a *patriotic* objection. It is that he has drawn away our attention from our own more noble native American trees, to waste it on this miserable pigtail of an Indiaman." The *New York Times* described it as a "filthy and worthless foreigner," aligning itself with the "Know-nothings," a far-right nativist and anti-immigrant party. The tree has gone through many lifecycles as a symbol— an exotic mark of class ascent in the early 19th Century,

a threat of immigrant invasion in the latter half of the 19th Century, a metaphor for resilience and uplift from urban poverty in the mid-20th Century. Reflecting on his time walking in Washington Square as a young child, Henry James recalled the characteristic odor of the Ailanthus as follows: "It was here that you took your first walks abroad, following the nursery-maid with unequal step and sniffing up the strange odour of the ailantus-trees which at that time formed the principal umbrage of the Square, and diffused an aroma that you were not yet critical enough to dislike as it deserved." The tree becomes, in James' novel, an ambivalent relationship— alternatively oppressive and freeing, corrupting and pure— reminiscent of the particularly olfactory terms that describe immigrant (particularly Jewish and East Asian) enclaves in the literature and public documents of the 19th and 20th Century.

This particular poem owes a debt to the following:

Eric L. Goldstein, *The Price of Whiteness: Jews, Race, and American Identity* (Princeton, 2008).

Catherine McNeur, "The Tree That Still Grows in Brooklyn, And Almost Everywhere Else." The Gotham Center for New York History, 2018.

2. These poems were written as documentations of taxi and Uber rides that I took to deliver poetry readings or to teach in Manhattan, Los Angeles, East Lansing, and Singapore. The drivers were all immigrants from South Asia— from Pakistan, Kerala, Bangladesh, and Punjab.

3. "അല്ലേ?" Malayalam, literally, "Is it not?" and colloquially "Isn't it?" Used as an invitation to agreement.

4. "amamma." Malayalam & Tamil. Literally, "grandmother."

5. "chetaa." Malayalam. Literally, "brother" and colloquially "bro" or "friend."

LANDSCAPES (AS PORTRAITS): OR THE POET AS CHILD-WITNESS TO U.S. & INDIAN IMPERIAL EXPANSIONS (1990-1994)

1. These poems are located at the intersection of the rise of anti-Kashmiri Freedom sentiment in India and the US-led Gulf War, which was the first war to be televised globally through the widespread imposition of cable news networks and the use of cameras attached to bombers. In 1990, our little township in India had decided to welcome American Television through cables and satellite. Indian children were to become the new and tender audiences for the strange romances enjoyed by the tanned upper-classes in *The Bold and the Beautiful* and the clumsy middle-classes in *America's Funniest Home Videos*. We were also to become the new audiences for Operation Desert Storm— our/their invasions into Iraq. In order for us to become audiences of this war and become initiated into an American caste-system, they had to find a way for a new god to course through the suburban landscape. They dug up our streets. They uprooted our trees. They pushed and ploughed over our pavements until the map of my childhood town looked like ruled paper on which to compose new, global images.

See also: Divya Victor/Karin Aue, "Sugar on the Gash." *The Margins/Asian American Writers Workshop*. July 2018.

MORE CURBS

1. A curb injury in equine patients refers to a cluster of soft tissue injuries in the plantar hock region, which changes the gait of horse.

2. The poems in this section owe a debt to information from the following sources (among many others):

Rana Sodhi & Harjit Sodhi, "Remembering Balbir Singh Sodhi, Sikh Man Killed in Post-9/11 Hate Crime." *StoryCorps*. September 14, 2018.

Tamar Levin, "Sikh Owner of Gas Station Is Fatally Shot in Rampage." *New York Times*. September 17, 2001.

Natsu Taylor Saito, *Settler Colonialism, Race, and the Law: Why Structural Racism Persists*. NYU Press, 2010.

Amitava Kumar, "Being Indian in Trump's America." *The New Yorker*. March 15, 2017.

Marc Santora, "Woman Is Charged with Murder as a Hate Crime in a Fatal Subway Push." *New York Times*. December 29, 2012.

Zayda Rivera and Paul Meara, "New Jersey Teens Yelled Racial Slurs at Black Girls but Did Not Urinate on Anyone at Football Game." *BET News*. November 4, 2019.

"2 teen boys charged with harassment, bias at high school football game." NJ.Com. October 19, 2019.

Nell Irvin Painter, "A Racist Attack Shows How Whiteness Evolves." *New York Times*. October 26, 2019.

PAVEMENT & FREQUENCY

1. saṃyuktākṣara. (Hindi, संयुक्ताक्षर) Literally, "a conjunct letter," a letter that can be connected to another letter.

2. व. Devanagari letter. IPA: /ʋə/, /wə/, /və/

3. य. Devanagari letter. IPA: /jə/

4. व्य. Conjoined (conjunct) form of व & य

5. ə. The Latin letter schwa.

6. ्. Devanagari diacritical mark which signals that the default vowel after a consonant is to be suppressed.

The poems in these sections are co-composed. I owe a debt to information from the following sources (among many others):

"Last of 5 charged in fatal Old Bridge beating case sentenced to 12 years in prison." NJ.Com. March 29, 2019.

Mast Radio, "Alka Sinha speaks on loss of her husband, sentencing day." YouTube Video. Oct 10, 2013.

ESTATES: LAST OFFICES CONCERNING THE CURBS OF THE BODY

1. ˘ Breve. A diacritical mark shaped like the lower curve of a circle. It signals a long vowel.
2. हम. Hindi, "us." Pronounced "hum."

3. ´ & `. Acute & Grave. Diacritical marks shaped like opposing sharp, angled strokes. They signal pitch.

4. विदेशी. Hindi, "foreigner." Pronounced "vi-day-shee."

5. ¸ Cedilla. A diacritical mark shaped like a little hook. It signals an altered pronunciation.

6. दुपट्टा. Hindi, "veil" or "scarf". Pronounced "du-putt-aa"

7. सांस. Hindi, "breath". Pronounced "sahn-ss," with the nasal stress on the "hn."

8. "a forehead aflame/with ghosts" references a poem from *Kith*, "No English. Indian. Walking," which (unbeknownst to me at the time) led to the writing of this book.

ACKNOWLEDGMENTS

The work and collaborative engagements related to *Curb* have been supported by Michigan State University's Humanities and Arts Research Program (HARP) Development grant, a commission from Colorado College, a seed grant for the MSU Digital Humanities and Literary Cognition Lab, and an Andrew Mellon Foundation "Just Futures" Grant.

Portions of this book first appeared as an artists' book which was commissioned, designed, and printed by Aaron Cohick of The Press at Colorado College, with a Clamshell box made by Further Other Book Works. The binding is a double-sided accordion-fold spine, with sewn-in chapbooks and fold-outs. The printing incorporates a traditional, carefully crafted approach to typography and letterpress printing; a complete reversal of those traditions through repetitive overprinting; and direct rubbings made from sidewalks and curbs, which imprint the pages with a textural trace of concrete. The book measures 12.5" x 8" (closed) and 12.5" x 13' (fully extended). Without the Aaron Cohick's CC commission, no iteration of *Curb* would have been possible.

Earlier versions of poems from this book have appeared in:

POETRY Magazine
The POETRY Foundation
CORDITE Review
The Capilano Review
Domain 22
Playgirl
jubilat
The Against Nature Journal

My poems are made through performance and I am grateful to the following editors/curators who helped me realize this book's poetics on an embodied stage: Aaron Cohick at Colorado College, Alessandro Porco at the University of North Carolina Wilmington, Andrea Abi-Karam & Rebecca Teich for the Segue Reading Series, Bellamy Mitchell at University of Chicago, the curators of FRIEZE Los Angeles, Jeffrey Pethybridge at Naropa University, Jessica Lowenthal at the Kelly Writers House, Kyle Dacuyan for The Poetry Project, Brian Teare & Jena Osman at Temple University, Joseph Mosconi & Andrew Maxwell at the Poetic Research Bureau, Michael Slosek & Katie Klocksin for PoetryNow at The Poetry Foundation, Sophia Hussain & Ken Chen at The Asian American Writers' Workshop (AAWW), Jeffrey Lependorf for The Flowchart Foundation.

I am indebted to friends and fellow poets for their patient reading of the materials in this book, and to my collaborators for their adventurous engagements that have made *Curb* so much more than an arrangement for codex. I am grateful to new and old friends for their company and insight during the scarier and the lonelier moments of composing, editing, parenting, teaching, advocating, and curating through a viral pandemic and an epidemic of police and extra-judicial violence. I am also thankful to elders in poetry who have laid the cool stones along the coal paths and who have helped me write about difficult things. *Curb* speaks in many tongues, and it could not have done so without the help of language experts and native speakers of Tamil, Malayalam, Arabic, French, Hindi, and Gujarati. Nightboat is the only home that could have truly held this book and seen its journey through with precision, patience, deep love for difficult texts. When I worked with the press' editors, publicists, and designers, I felt that my poetry was real to them and that made it more real to me. Bookmakers are the alchemists of language's dreams. *Thank you*: Al Filreis, Amarnath Ravva, Andrea

Abi-Karam, Bhanu Kapil, Brandon Brown, CA Conrad, Caelan Nardone, Claudia Rankine, CJ Martin, Carolyn Chen, Cathy Park Hong, Craig Dworkin, Dawn Lundy Martin, Dee Morris, Don Mee Choi, Douglas Kearney, Ellen McCallum, Eric Schmaltz, Gabrielle Civil, Greenlee Brown, Hannah Ensor, HR Hegnauer, Jaye Elijah, Jeff Wray, Jena Osman, Jessica Lowenthal, Jessica Stokes, Jordan Scott, Jose Clarence, José Felipe Alvergue, Josh Yumibe, Julia Bloch, Julian Chambliss, Juliet Guzzetta, Julie Carr, Justus Nieland, Karin Aue, Kristin Mahoney, Lindsay Turner, Lindsey Boldt, Lyn Goeringer, Mahesh Sharma, Marwa Helal, Melissa Wright, Michael Nardone, Mrigaa Sethi, M. NourbeSe Philip, Prageeta Sharma, Rachel Blau DuPlessis, Rachel Zolf, Robin Silbergleid, Sara Wedell, Sawako Nakayasu, Serena Chopra, Shivram Gopinath, Stephen Motika, Swarnavel Eswaran Pillai, Tamar Boyadjian, Tessa Paneth-Pollack, Vivek Vellanki, Yomaira Figueroa, Zarena Aslami; Jolene Sonia Costa, Karen Koh, and Sarifah Azlin for being there many oceans away; Zameen's babysitters & teachers (BSJ, BH, MC, PM, MLM) and my family's therapists (KM, SS); my superlative colleagues at Michigan State University and the University of Pennsylvania's *Jacket2*. Thank you, Joshua Lam—my first and staunchest reader; thank you Mom, Dad, Paati—you are my first and eternal crew on this tiny boat home. Thank you, my Michigan families-by-choice, for being *terra sana* and for keeping theatre, music, and books alive. Thank you, Zameen Martina Victor-Lam, for making me your Ammi—you are my most daring/darling line break, in the flesh.

Divya Victor is the author of *Kith*, *Natural Subjects* (Winner of the Bob Kaufman Award), *Unsub*, and *Things To Do With Your Mouth*. Her work has been collected in numerous venues, including, more recently, *BOMB*, the New Museum's *The Animated Reader*, *Crux: Journal of Conceptual Writing*, *The Best American Experimental Writing*, POETRY, and *boundary2*. Her work has been translated into French, German, Spanish, and Czech. She teaches at Michigan State University.

NIGHTBOAT BOOKS

Nightboat Books, a nonprofit organization, seeks to develop audiences for writers whose work resists convention and transcends boundaries. We publish books rich with poignancy, intelligence, and risk. Please visit nightboat.org to learn about our titles and how you can support our future publications.

The following individuals have supported the publication of this book. We thank them for their generosity and commitment to the mission of Nightboat Books:

Kazim Ali
Anonymous (4)
Jean C. Ballantyne
The Robert C. Brooks Revocable Trust
Amanda Greenberger
Rachel Lithgow
Anne Marie Macari
Elizabeth Madans
Elizabeth Motika
Thomas Shardlow
Benjamin Taylor
Jerrie Whitfield & Richard Motika

In addition, this book has been made possible, in part, by grants from the National Endowment for the Arts, the New York City Department of Cultural Affairs in partnership with the City Council, and the New York State Council on the Arts Literature Program.